Introductic

M000291112

Your special friends deserve unique greetings, and these quilted postcards provide just the answer. Following the easy design patterns in this book, you can quickly turn plain card stock into cheerful, colorful postcards for any occasion, and you can actually send them through the mail!

All it takes to complete the cards is your choice of bright and lively fabrics, a small amount of thin batting and a little sewing.

Imagine how surprised your friends will be when they receive your thoughtful, decorative greeting in the mail or attached to a present at a special event!

Table of Contents

General Directions

The following materials and instructions are needed for all projects:

Materials

Card stock, cut to 4 x 6 inches
Fabric, such as cotton, flannel, sheer fabric or lace
Note: Test delicate fabrics (such as organza, silk, etc.) for compatibility with heat, which will be required for fusing.

Cotton batting
Note: Our photographed postcards were made with Warm & Natural needled cotton batting.

Lightweight paper-backed fusible web, such as HeatnBond Lite
Press cloth
Ironing board and iron
Scissors
Rotary cutter and mat for trimming (optional)
Sewing machine
Sewing thread
Tracing paper
Pins
Sharp pencil
Embellishments of your choice, such as beads, buttons, brads, ribbon, lace, specialty threads and paint
Glue (see pattern)
Glue stitck (optional)

Fusing the Pieces

Trace one of each pattern piece and background selected onto paper side of fusible web leaving at least ¼ inch between pieces. Mark pattern details to assist in placement of fabric pieces on background. For lettering placement, this can be done before pieces are assembled. *Hint: If you want a particular motif from the fabric to be centered in the design piece, hold fabric up to light and mark placement.*

Cut out fusible web pattern pieces ⅛ inch larger than pattern.

Fuse to wrong side of fabric following manufacturer's instructions. *Note: Be careful not to iron the wrong side of the fusible web or it will stick to the bottom of your iron, requiring cleaning with an iron cleaner. Use of a press cloth is also helpful for keeping your iron clean.*

Cut out pattern pieces and background piece.

Peel off fusible web paper from background fabric and fuse to a piece of batting. Trim to match fabric size.

Peel off fusible web paper from each pattern piece. **Arrange** pieces on the background fabric, referring to photo and pattern for placement. You can tack pieces lightly with a glue stick or by slightly touching the tip of the iron in the center of the fabric.

When satisfied with placement, fuse in place.

Stitch the Pieces

Machine-stitch with a narrow satin stitch around the pattern pieces.

Quilt according to individual instructions or as desired.

Embellishing

When stitching ribbons, pin the ribbon to start, and then twist and turn the ribbon while stitching through it.

To add brads, make a small hole through fabric and batting with a large needle or the point of a seam ripper where you have marked the placement. Poke brad through and flatten back of prongs. *Note: Do not iron directly on top of brads.*

To add buttons, beads or charms, do the machine quilting first, and then sew on the embellishments before fusing the quilt to the card stock. If you prefer to glue on the embellishments, wait until after the quilt has been fused to the card.

Finishing the Postcard

Fuse Turn piece batting side up and add strips of fusible web; place on top of card stock and press. (Or you may choose to lightly tack the 4 x 6-inch piece directly to the card stock with a glue stick.)

Trim quilt fabric even with postcard.

Stitch outside edge with overcast stitch or simple zigzag stitch.

Glue on any final embellishments.

Mailing the Postcard

Postcard quilts can be sent through the mail just like any other postcards. However, if you have added beads, sequins or other embellishments, you may wish to have it hand-cancelled. This will require extra postage.

First class post cards have the following size requirements:
No smaller than:
3½" high x 5" long x 0.0007" thick
No larger than:
4½" high x 6" long x 0.016" thick

If you prefer to send the postcard quilt in an envelope, it may require extra postage, depending on its weight, and may need to be hand-canceled if it is thickly embellished.

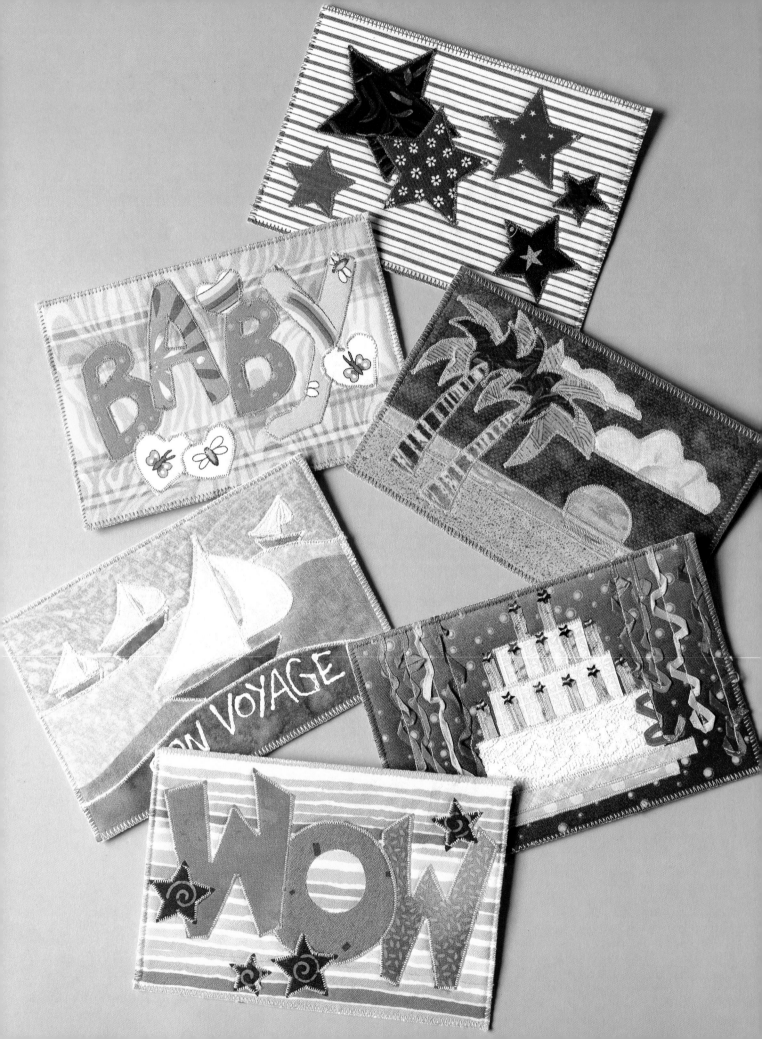

Birthday Greetings

Note: *Refer to General Directions (page 3) for general material requirements and instructions common to all projects.*

Design pattern is on page 20.

Fabric Suggestions

Background—dk blue print
Cake—white-on-white print
Platter—two gold prints
Candles—gold texture
Cake trim—lace (1" x 3"-wide)
(optional)
Flames—13 (5mm) star sequins
Ribbons—⅓ yd ⅛"-wide each yellow and orange
         —½ yd (⅛"-wide) each pink and red
Thread—coordinating and contrasting colors

Special Instructions

1. Optional lace trim can be fused to cake piece before fusing cake piece to background.

2. Candles can be fused onto fabric as one piece, and then cut for placement on cake.

3. Sew on star sequins by hand before fusing quilted design to card stock.

WOW or MOM

Note: *Refer to General Directions (page 3) for general material requirements and instructions common to all projects.*

Design pattern is on page 20.

Fabric Suggestions

Background—med pastel stripe
Letters—bright green, purple and pink
Stars—dk blue
Thread—coordinating and contrasting colors

Special Instructions

1. Lightly tack letters and stars in place to arrange.

2. Referring to photo, overlap letters and stars.

Baby Time

Note: Refer to General Directions (page 3) for general material requirements and instructions common to all projects.

Design pattern is on page 21.

Fabric Suggestions

Background—pastel stripes
Letters—pink print and green print
Hearts—baby print, cut so motifs are centered in hearts
Thread—coordinating and contrasting colors

Special Instructions

1. Lightly tack letters and hearts in place to arrange.

2. Referring to photo, overlap letters and hearts.

Reach for the Stars

Note: Refer to General Directions (page 3) for general material requirements and instructions common to all projects.

Design pattern is on page 21.

Fabric Suggestions

Background—blue-and-white stripe
Stars—four blues and two reds
Thread—coordinating and contrasting colors

Special Instructions

When arranging design, tack stars in place, overlapping two large stars as shown on design pattern.

Life's a Beach

Note: *Refer to General Directions (page 3) for general material requirements and instructions common to all projects.*

Design pattern is on page 22.

Fabric Suggestions

Background—dk blue
Water—lt blue
Sand—lt tan texture
Palm fronds—lt green and dk green
Note: *Cut fronds from each fabric as one piece.*
Tree trunks—neutral stripe
Sun—orange/pink texture
Clouds—pink
Thread—coordinating and contrasting colors

Special Instructions

1. Lightly tack water and sand to background. Add clouds, lt green fronds, dk green fronds and tree trunks.

2. Tuck sun under water as shown on design pattern.

3. Add quilting to form reflection in water.

Set Sail

Note: *Refer to General Directions (page 3) for general material requirements and instructions common to all projects.*

Design pattern is on page 22.

Fabric Suggestions

Background—lt blue texture
Foreground—med blue
Sheer top layer—white organza, 1½"-wide ribbon or fabric
Sails—white and off-white
Boats—red, orange, lavender and green
Thread—coordinating and contrasting colors
Tracing paper
Ink or paint

Special Instructions

1. Trace words onto tracing paper, reverse tracing paper, and then trace onto right side of foreground fabric. For dark fabrics, it will help to hold them up to a window or a light box.

2. Fuse med blue foreground fabric to lt blue texture fabric background, and then fuse sheer layer on top.

3. Add boats and sails.

4. Follow General Directions on page 3 for machine-stitching sheer top layer, boats, and sails.

4. Use permanent ink or acrylic paint to highlight words after completing card.

Sending Love

Note: *Refer to General Directions (page 3) for general material requirements and instructions common to all projects.*

Design pattern is on page 23.

Fabric Suggestions

Background—pink-and-green print
Stripe—med green
Letters—dk pink-and-lavender print
Thread—coordinating and contrasting colors

Special Instructions

1. Since heavy stitching of the letters on top of the green strip may tend to shrink or draw in the fabric, make sure green strip measures an extra ⅛" on the left and right sides.

2. Fuse stripe to background and satin-stitch edges before fusing letters in place.

3. Trim background to card.

For My Valentine

Note: *Refer to General Directions (page 3) for general material requirements and instructions common to all projects.*

Design pattern is on page 23.

Fabric Suggestions

Background—dk red heart print
Hearts—five shades of lt–med pink
1"-wide lace flower (optional)
Fabric glue (for optional flower)
Thread—coordinating and contrasting colors

Special Instructions

1. Referring to photo, tuck one large heart under the other.

2. Glue optional lace flower to finished card.

Let's Do Coffee

Note: *Refer to General Directions (page 3) for general material requirements and instructions common to all projects.*

Design pattern is on page 24.

Fabric Suggestions

Background—red texture
Foreground—brown
Cups—lt blue, dk blue, lt tan and med tan
Stars—gold
Thread—coordinating and contrasting colors

Special Instructions

1. Fuse foreground to background.

2. Cut basic shape of each cup from light-color fabrics, and then cut smaller pieces from darker-color fabrics.

3. Fuse smaller pieces to cups.

4. Tack cups lightly until stars are placed, tucking stars and tall coffee cup underneath as shown on design pattern.

Basket of Grapes

Note: *Refer to General Direction (page 3) for general materials requirements and instructions common to all projects.*

Design pattern is on page 24.

Fabric Suggestions

Background—lt gold print
Basket—med green large print
Basket handle—med green small print
Filler—med print of grapes, leaves or desired pattern
Thread—coordinating and contrasting colors

Special Instructions

1. Iron fusible web onto areas of filler fabric. Cut out.

2. Lightly tack basket and handle in place. Arrange filler so that grapes and leaves are either tucked under, or appear to spill out of, basket pieces.

3. Tuck handles behind basket, as shown on design pattern.

Dragonfly Note

Note: *Refer to General Directions (page 3) for general material requirements and instructions common to all projects.*

Design pattern is on page 25.

Fabric Suggestions

Background—lt blue
Flower front layer—orange
Flower back layer—dk rust print
Flower center—gold
Stem—dk green
Leaf—med green print
Dragonflies—green, blue and gold prints
Thread—coordinating and contrasting colors
Tracing paper

Special Instructions

1. Mark placement for dragonflies antennae by tracing the antennae onto tracing paper; reverse tracing paper, and then trace onto right side of background fabric. For dark fabrics, it will help to hold them up to a window or a light box.

2. Referring to design pattern, fuse back layer of flower petals and stem to background, tucking stem beneath flower, and then fuse front layer of flower and flower center.

3. Fuse leaf and dragonfly wings, tucking upper wings under lower wings. Fuse dragonfly body to match placement of antennae.

Flower Basket

Note: *Refer to General Directions (page 3) for general material requirements and instructions common to all projects.*

Design pattern is on page 25.

Fabric Suggestions

Background—pink print
Basket and handle—med dk rose large print, texture
Filler flowers—med to large floral print
Leaves—med and dk green
Thread—coordinating and contrasting colors

Special Instructions

1. Iron fusible web to desired areas of filler fabrics. Cut out.

2. Lightly tack basket and handle in place. Arrange filler fabrics so it appears to spill out of basket piece.

3. Add leaves among the filler items, tucking underneath.

4. Tuck handles underneath basket, as shown on design pattern.

Festive Poinsettia

Note: *Refer to General Directions (page 3) for general material requirements and instructions common to all projects.*

Design pattern is on page 26.

Fabric Suggestions

Background—dk green
Poinsettia petals—dk pink and red
Poinsettia center—yellow-green
Center decoration—8 flower brads, small buttons or
   beads (optional)
Glue (if using buttons or beads)
Thread—coordinating and contrasting colors

Special Instructions

1. For two-toned petals, cut two strips of each petal fabric 1" x 18". Stitch together lengthwise, press and fuse to fusible fabric.

2. Cut out each petal, centering the seam. Number petals on fusible backing to keep them in order.

3. Lightly tack green center, then arrange petals in numerical order, tucking under center.

4. Attach brads after quilting but before fusing to card stock. If using buttons or beads instead of brads, glue in place after completing postcard.

Holiday Wreath

Note: *Refer to General Directions (page 3) for general material requirements and instructions common to all projects.*

Design pattern is on page 26.

Fabric Suggestions

Background—lt gold
Wreath shape—dk green
Holly leaves—3 med green prints or solids
Bow—18" (¼"-wide) red ribbon
Thread—coordinating and contrasting colors

Special Instructions

1. Fuse wreath shape to background.

2. Referring to photo, arrange holly leaves, starting at top and overlapping to lower edge of wreath.

3. Tie ribbon into bow, pin in place and stitch down bow.

4. Stitch ribbon tails while twisting into desired shape.

Jolly Snowman

Note: Refer to General Directions (page 3) for general material requirements and instructions common to all projects.

Design pattern is on page 27.

Fabric Suggestions

Background—blue texture
Snowman—white texture
Scarf—red print and green print
Hat—black
Hatband—dk gray
Holly—holly print
Nose—orange
Eyes—black or dk gray
Mouth—4 mini brads, black
Thread—coordinating and contrasting colors

Special Instructions

1. After fusing pieces, add highlights to eyes with narrow zigzag stitch or acrylic paint.

2. Referring to photo, add quilting lines to eyes, nose, and scarf.

3. Attach brads before fusing to card stock. Do not iron directly on the brads.

Happy Red Hat

Note: Refer to General Directions (page 3) for general material requirements and instructions common to all projects.

Design pattern is on page 27.

Fabric Suggestions

Background—lt cream print
Hat—lt red, med red, dk red
Hatband—purple
Decoration—18" (⅛"-wide) purple ribbon
　　　　　—18" (¾"-wide) gold braid
Thread—coordinating and contrasting colors

Special Instructions

1. Attach gold braid with fusible fabric or fabric glue and then fuse hat and hatband.

2. To add ribbon decoration, tie bow and stitch in place, and then stitch the ribbon tails, twisting and curving as you stitch.

It's Halloween

Note: *Refer to General Directions (page 3) for general material requirements and instructions common to all projects.*

Design pattern is on page 28.

Fabric Suggestions

Background—green
Cat—purple
Ear and nose—pink
Hat—black
Pumpkins—orange
Leaf—dk green
Faces—white
Stem—brown
Hatband—12" (⅛"-wide) orange ribbon
Eyes—6 black mini brads
Thread—coordinating and contrasting colors

Special Instructions

1. Fuse face to background. Trace cat whiskers onto tracing paper; reverse tracing paper and trace onto right side of cat face and background fabric.

2. For ribbon hatband, tie bow in center of ribbon and pin to hat. Stitch bow knot first, and then stitch the ribbon tails, twisting and curving as you stitch.

3. Before fusing to card stock, but after quilting, attach brads. Do not iron directly over brads.

4. Stitch whiskers.

5. Fuse to card stock.

Halloween Pumpkins

Note: *Refer to General Directions (page 3) for general material requirements and instructions common to all projects.*

Design pattern is on page 28.

Fabric Suggestions

Background—Halloween print
Pumpkins—3 shades of orange
Leaves—2 shades of green
Faces—yellow and purple
Stems—brown
Eyes—6 mini brads
Thread—coordinating and contrasting colors

Special Instructions

1. Lightly tack pieces in place until all pieces are arranged.

2. Referring to design pattern, tuck stems under pumpkins and overlap pumpkins and leaves as shown.

3. Attach brads after quilting but before fusing to card stock. Do not iron directly over brads.

House to House

Note: *Refer to General Direction (page 3) for general materials requirements and instructions common to all projects.*

Design pattern is on page 29.

Fabric Suggestions

Background—lt blue
Red house—two shades of red
White house—white print
Roofs—brown texture
Chimneys—red and dk red
Windows—yellow and dk gold
Doors—dk blue and white
Grass—med green
Sidewalks—brown
Thread—coordinating and contrasting colors

Special Instructions

1. Fuse grass to background fabric first, and then add houses, sidewalks and details.

2. Tuck chimneys underneath roofs as shown on design pattern.

Sunshine Wishes

Note: *Refer to General Directions (page 3) for general material requirements and instructions common to all projects.*

Design pattern is on page 29.

Fabric Suggestions

Background—lt blue
Sun rays—dk orange
Center—yellow
Cheeks—pink
Mouth—dk pink
Eyes—2 (5mm) black mini brads
Thread—coordinating and contrasting colors
Tracing paper

Special Instructions

1. Trace face onto tracing paper, reverse tracing paper, and then trace onto right side of foreground fabric. For dark fabrics, it will help to hold them up to a window or a light box.

2. Cut sun rays in one piece and fuse to background, and then fuse center and face pieces.

3. Attach brads after quilting but before fusing to card stock. Do not iron directly over brads.

On the Road

Note: *Refer to General Directions (page 3) for general material requirements and instructions common to all projects.*

Design pattern is on page 30.

Fabric Suggestions

Background—lt blue texture
Foreground—lt green print
Mountains—purple
Trees—3 shades of green
Tree trunks—med brown
Road—dk brown
Centerline—lt-and-dk striped
Thread—coordinating and contrasting colors

Special Instructions

1. Fuse mountain and foreground shapes to background first, and then add road, stripe and trees.

2. Referring to photo, add quilting to form cloud and perspective lines.

Wish You Were Here

Note: *Refer to General Directions (page 3) for general material requirements and instructions common to all projects.*

Design pattern is on page 30.

Fabric Suggestions

Background—lt blue texture
Foreground—dk green print
Mountains—purple
Trees—3 shades of green
Tree trunk on large tree—brown
Thread—coordinating and contrasting colors

Special Instructions

1. Fuse mountain and foreground shapes to background and then **a**dd trees.

2. Referring to photo, create "breeze" lines with quilting.

Spring Leaf

Note: *Refer to General Directions (page 3) for general material requirements and instructions common to all projects.*

Design pattern is on page 31.

Fabric Suggestions

Background—lt gold
Frame—med and dk green print
Leaf—yellow-green
Flowers—magenta and peach
Centers—yellow
Stems and leaves—dk green
Thread—coordinating and contrasting colors

Special Instructions

1. Cut flowers as one piece, not four petals.

2. Fuse frame pieces to background before adding leaf and flowers.

3. Referring to pattern, lightly tack leaf in place, then arrange flowers and stems, tucking them underneath leaf.

4. Referring to photo, quilt along stitching line in center of leaf.

Windsor Knot

Note: *Refer to General Directions (page 3) for general material requirements and instructions common to all projects.*

Design pattern is on page 31.

Fabric Suggestions

Background—lt blue
Ties—5 prints, at least 1 stripe
Tie knots—5 coordinating prints, or use same fabric as tie
Tie pins—2 (4mm) rhinestones (optional)
Gem-Tac glue for optional tie pins
Thread—coordinating and contrasting colors

Special Instructions

1. Tuck tie knots under ties if using separate fabrics.

2. Stitch along quilting lines.

3. If adding optional rhinestones, refer to photo and glue with Gem-Tac after card has been completed. Do not iron directly over rhinestones.

Birthday Greetings DESIGN PATTERN

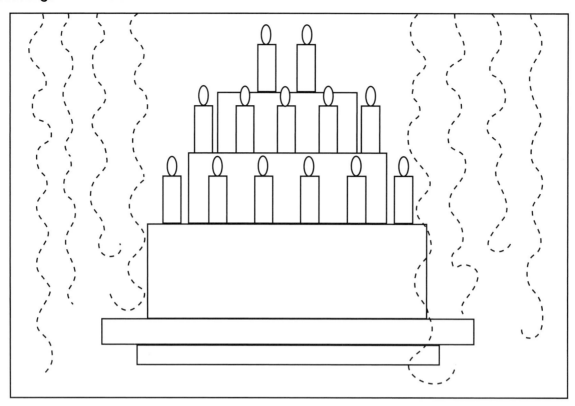

WOW or MOM DESIGN PATTERN

Baby Time DESIGN PATTERN

Reach for the Stars DESIGN PATTERN

Life's a Beach DESIGN PATTERN

Set Sail DESIGN PATTERN

Sending Love DESIGN PATTERN

For My Valentine DESIGN PATTERN

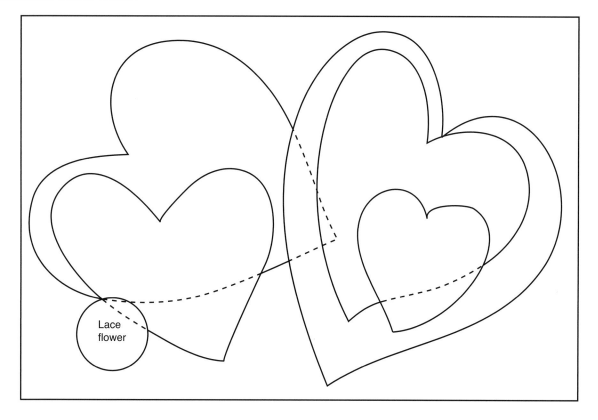

Lace flower

Let's Do Coffee DESIGN PATTERN

Basket of Grapes DESIGN PATTERN

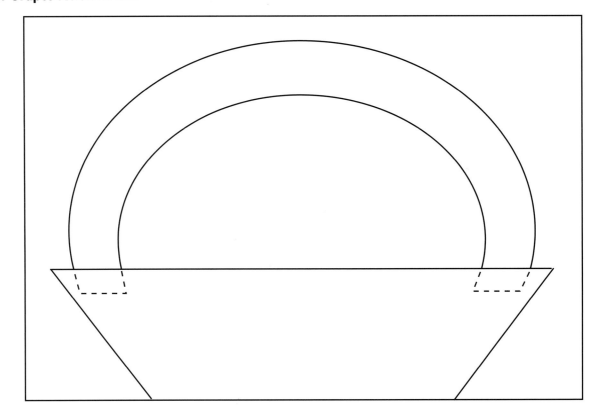

Dragonfly Note DESIGN PATTERN

Flower Basket DESIGN PATTERN

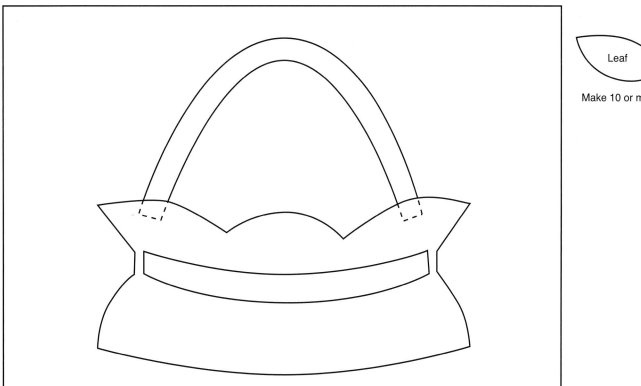

Leaf

Make 10 or more

Festive Poinsettia DESIGN PATTERN

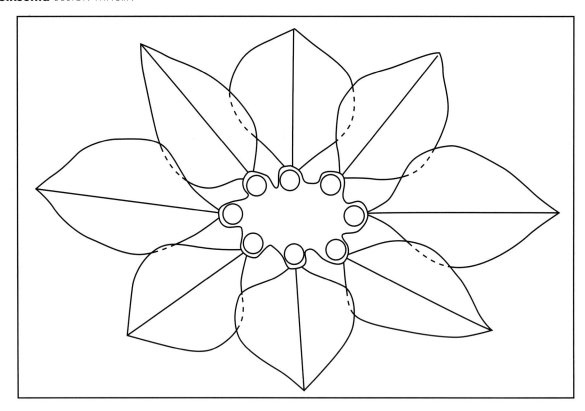

Holiday Wreath DESIGN PATTERN

Make 10

Jolly Snowman DESIGN PATTERN

Happy Red Hat DESIGN PATTERN

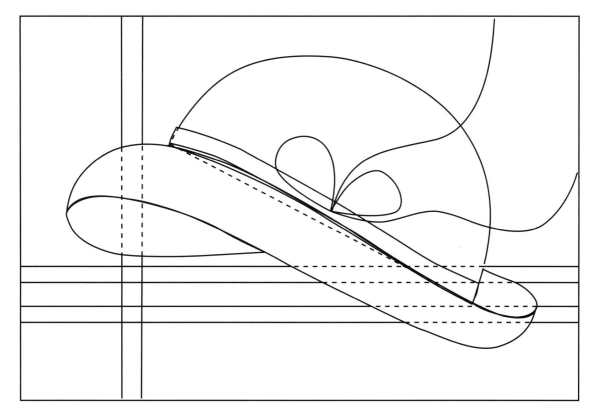

It's Halloween DESIGN PATTERN

Halloween Pumpkins DESIGN PATTERN

House to House DESIGN PATTERN

Sunshine Wishes DESIGN PATTERN

stitching lines

On the Road DESIGN PATTERN

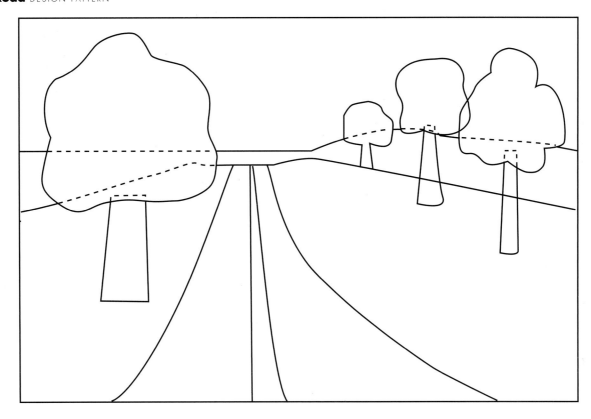

Wish You Were Here DESIGN PATTERN

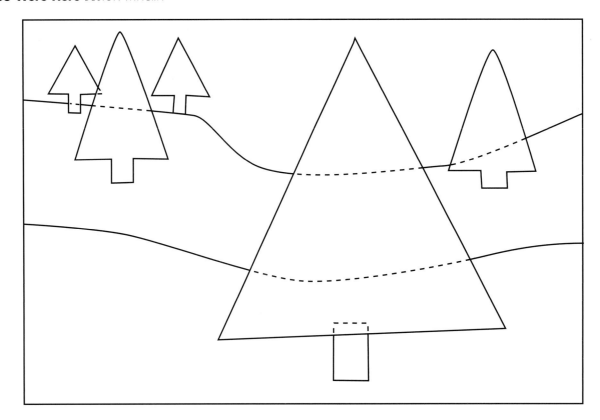

Spring Leaf DESIGN PATTERN

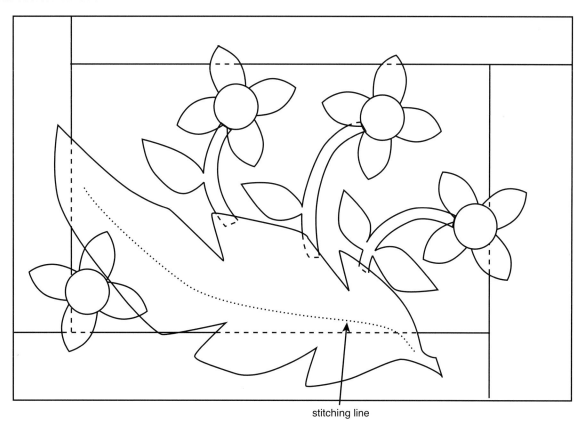

stitching line

Windsor Knot DESIGN PATTERN

stitching lines

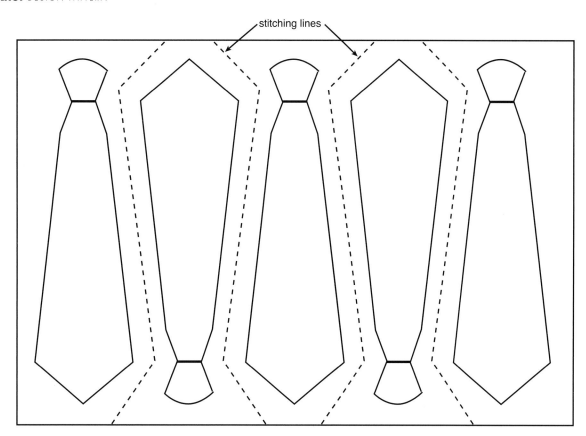

We wish to thank the following companies who generously supplied products for the projects:

Gütermann of America: 100% cotton sewing thread
Therm O Web: HeatnBond Lite iron-on adhesive
Northcott Silk Inc.: cotton fabrics

DRG Publishing
306 East Parr Road
Berne, IN 46711
©2005 American School of Needlework

TOLL-FREE ORDER LINE or to request a free catalog (800) 582-6643
Customer Service (800) 282-6643, **Fax** (800) 882-6643

Visit AnniesAttic.com.